AN ABBEY THEATRE PRODUCTION

MOLIÈRE'S
TARTUFFE

a new version by
Frank McGuinness

First performed on 3 March 2023
at the Abbey Theatre, Dublin

CREATIVES

MONSIEUR LOYAL	Amy Conroy
MARIANE	Emma Rose Creaner
TARTUFFE	Ryan Donaldson
DAMIS	Naoise Dunbar
DORINE	Pauline Hutton
ORGON	Frank McCusker
ELMIRE	Aislín McGuckin
FILIPOTE	Clare McKenna
VALERE	Emmanuel Okoye
PERNELLE	Geraldine Plunkett
OFFICER	Darragh Shannon
CLEANTE	Kevin Trainor

Written by	Molière
In a new version by	Frank McGuinness
Director	Caitríona McLaughlin
Set & Costume Designer	Katie Davenport
Lighting Designer	Sinéad Wallace
Composer & Sound Designer	Philip Stewart
Movement Director	Paula O'Reilly
Voice Director	Andrea Ainsworth
Casting Director	Sarah Jones
Production Dramaturg	Tanya Dean
Hair & Makeup Designer	Leonard Daly
Associate Composer & Sound Designer	Jane Deasy
Assistant Lighting Designer	Matt Burke
Publicity Photo	Finn Richards
Publicity Photo Art Direction	AAD

PROGRAMME NOTE

Caitríona McLaughlin
Tartuffe *Director and Abbey Theatre Artistic Director, January 2023*

In addition to capturing the zeitgeist, great artists also have the gift of clairvoyance: they write the future. Great comic writers go one step further: they encode the DNA of their own anarchic laughter into our present, a present that would be unrecognisable to them apart from a few salient details – the persistence of hypocrisy as a tool for social advancement, for example, and of saying one thing and meaning another. The play is also about power, the power of money, of sex, and of patriarchal control and how they can be manipulated into new and disguised forms. Who could be a more apt avatar of our post-factual conspiracy-theorised twenty-first-century world than the figure of Tartuffe, who through pious pronouncements and imposed restrictions shames Orgon's household into a confused chaos of accusation and counter-accusation, thereby enabling a smokescreen behind which he can pilfer and philander with impunity? What fits the comic anarchy of our age better than the tart, acerbic genius of Molière?

Molière probably didn't know he was inadvertently writing about twenty-first-century Ireland, but Frank McGuinness certainly did. Frank has channelled the comic spirit, alacrity, bite, and gameplay of Tartuffe with a forensic precision and directness, underscored with a lash of his Ulster tongue and held within the controlled strictures of rhyming couplets. There's something surprisingly satisfying in the complexity and nuance both Molière and McGuinness achieve with a pair of lines that rhyme – an object lesson in compression and precision for all who express themselves within the 240 characters of your average tweet.

In an age where content is king, a mantra that powers keyboard warriors across the globe, meaning can get lost in the fog of culture wars. Daily, almost on the hour, we see governmental hypocrisy and corporate malfeasance exposed, politicians caught flouting the very edicts they decree we should abide by, and various cultural commentariat revealed to have feet of clay. Between two heartbeats, our pop stars, authors, and sultans of reality TV are swiftly deposed when a wrong-footed tweet or online video detonates across the socials. In seconds, and with dizzying velocity, reputations are shredded.

In *Tartuffe*, Molière slows this process down for us, and we see this mechanism laid bare. A lying hypocrite is unmasked by an all-seeing king and promptly cancelled. He had been cancelled before by his own tribe, when he lost his aristocratic entitlement, and has now reinvented himself as a destitute and abject saint. His previous wealth and entitlement privileged him with political and cultural currency, but he has now – with a Bowie-like transformation – created another form of currency amongst his liberal-minded converts: the currency of shame. Shame, still profoundly Irish, is a powerful emotion that can fundamentally alter a person because it is projected outwards, unlike guilt, which turns the gaze inside. If used on the susceptible, as Tartuffe does with Orgon, it dissembles. But Tartuffe is then cancelled a second time, by a higher authority than his aristocratic tribe, the king. Thus, fortunes are lost, lives are ruined, and 'truths slaved'.

Within this tight compass of imaginative folly, Molière creates a comic universe that delights and surprises. The delight comes not because previously hidden and unknown parts of human endeavour are revealed to the audience, but rather in *how* Molière reveals it, and *how* he contains and corrals the action – his sheer kinetic virtuosity – which Frank here has renewed and freshly minted. The surprise is that the trick is still *possible*. The best plays show us what it means to be human, and the comic playwrights who endure are those who reveal ourselves *to* ourselves through the laughter of recognition, which disarms us. They tell us things that are essentially unfunny because they are a serious matter but make us laugh at the sheer chutzpah of it, the desperation of it, the mess of it. If Molière holds up a mirror to nature, then it is a mirror in a cheap hotel room. The furnishings might look fancy, but deep down we know it's all a trick of the light. We catch a glimpse of our reflection out of the corner of our eye; we don't like it, but we smile in recognition. We know it looks like us before the Instagram filters.

ABBEY THEATRE AMHARCLANN NA MAINISTREACH

As Ireland's national theatre, the Abbey Theatre's ambition is to enrich the cultural lives of everyone with a curiosity for and interest in Irish theatre, stories, artists and culture. Courage and imagination are at the heart of our storytelling, while inclusivity, diversity and equality are at the core of our thinking. Led by Co-Directors Caitríona McLaughlin (Artistic Director) and Mark O'Brien (Executive Director), the Abbey Theatre celebrates both the rich canon of Irish dramatic writing and the potential of future generations of Irish theatre artists.

Ireland has a rich history of theatre and playwriting and extraordinary actors, designers and directors. Artists are at the heart of this organisation, with Marina Carr and Conor McPherson as Senior Associate Playwrights and Caroline Byrne as Associate Director. We also work with four Resident Directors – Gea Gojak, Claire O'Reilly, Laura Sheeran and Colm Summers.

Our stories teach us what it is to belong, what it is to be excluded and to exclude. Artistically our programme is built around two questions: 'who were we, and who are we now?' We interrogate our classical canon with an urgency about what makes it speak to this moment. On our stages we find and champion new voices and new ways of seeing, our purpose – to identify combinations of characters we are yet to meet, having conversations we are yet to hear.

abbeytheatre.ie

ABBEY THEATRE SUPPORTERS

PROGRAMME PARTNERS

CORPORATE GUARDIANS

Bloomberg

Irish Life

GOLD AMBASSADORS
Behaviour and Attitudes
Ecclesiastical

HOSPITALITY PARTNERS
The Westbury Hotel

SILVER AMBASSADORS
Trocadero

DIRECTORS' CIRCLE
Tony Ahearne
Pat Butlers
The Cielinski Family
Deirdre Finan
Janice Flynn
Elisabeth and Conor Kehoe
Dr. Frances Ruane
Susan and Denis Tinsley

SILVER PATRONS
Frances Britton
Catherine Byrne
Tommy Gibbons
Dr. John Keane
Andrew Mackey
Eugenie Mackey
Eugene Magee
Gerard and Liv McNaughton
The Kathleen Murphy Foundation
Andrew and Delyth Parkes

Patrons who wish to remain anonymous.
**We thank all our generous supporters for
their ongoing support.**

BECOME A SUPPORTER OR CORPORATE
GUARDIAN OF THE ABBEY THEATRE
AND HELP US TO BRING INSPIRATIONAL
WORK TO OUR STAGES, SCHOOLS, AND
TO DISENFRANCHISED COMMUNITIES
THROUGHOUT IRELAND.

Our mission is to nurture a love for the art form for the
generations to come, mentoring new talent and giving
voice to all of Ireland's citizens. If you'd like to support us
in our work, please contact: **marie.lawlor@abbeytheatre.ie**

Tartuffe

A VERSION BY FRANK MCGUINNESS

Molière (1622–73) was born Jean-Baptiste Poquelin, son of a prosperous upholsterer of Paris. Molière was meant to succeed his father in the service of the King. However, in 1643 he changed his surname and joined a family of actors, the Béjarts. Encouraged by their touring success the group returned to Paris and performed in front of Louis XIV and his Court. The success of his farce *Le Docteur Amoureux* gave the group the opportunity to share a theatre at the Petit-Bourbon with an Italian company, and here Molière's reputation was established. His plays include *L'Ecole des Femmes* (1662), *Dom Juan* (1665), *Tartuffe* (written 1664, produced 1669), *Le Misanthrope* (1666), *Le Bourgeois Gentilhomme* (1671), *Les Femmes Savantes* (1673) and *Le Malade Imaginaire* (1673).

Born in Donegal, Frank McGuinness lives in Dublin and is Professor Emeritus in Creative Writing at University College Dublin. His plays include *The Factory Girls* (1982), *Baglady* (1985), *Observe the Sons of Ulster Marching Towards the Somme* (1985), *Innocence* (1986), *Carthaginians* (1988), *Mary and Lizzie* (1989), *The Bread Man* (1991), *Someone Who'll Watch Over Me* (1992), *The Bird Sanctuary* (1994), *Mutabilitie* (1997), *Dolly West's Kitchen* (1999), *Gates of Gold* (2002), *Speaking Like Magpies* (2005), *There Came a Gypsy Riding* (2007), *Greta Garbo Came to Donegal* (2010), *The Match Box* (2012), *The Hanging Gardens* (2013), *The Visiting Hour* (2021) and *Dinner With Groucho* (2022). Among his many widely staged versions are *Rosmersholm* (1987), *Peer Gynt* (1988), *Hedda Gabler* (1994), *A Doll's House* (1997), *The Lady from the Sea* (2008), *Oedipus* (2008), *Helen* (2009), *Ghosts* (2010), *John Gabriel Borkman* (2010), *Damned by Despair* (2012) and *The Dead* (2012).

MOLIÈRE

Tartuffe

a new version by
Frank McGuinness

from a literal translation by
Derval Conroy

faber

First published in 2023
by Faber and Faber Limited
74–77 Great Russell Street
London WC1B 3DA

Typeset by Brighton Gray
Printed and bound in the UK by CPI Group (Ltd), Croydon CR0 4YY

This version of *Tartuffe* is based on a literal translation by Derval Conroy,
French Department, UCD School of Languages, Cultures and Linguistics

A CIP record for this book
is available from the British Library

978-0-571-38483-9

2 4 6 8 10 9 7 5 3 1

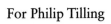

For Philip Tilling

Tartuffe in this adaptation was first performed on 3 March 2023 at the Abbey Theatre, Dublin, with the following cast:

Monsieur Loyal Amy Conroy
Mariane Emma Rose Creaner
Tartuffe Ryan Donaldson
Damis Naoise Dunbar
Dorine Pauline Hutton
Orgon Frank McCusker
Elmire Aislín McGuckin
Filipote Clare McKenna
Valere Emmanuel Okoye
Pernelle Geraldine Plunkett
Officer Darragh Shannon
Cleante Kevin Trainor

Director Caitríona McLaughlin
Set & Costume Designer Katie Davenport
Lighting Designer Sinéad Wallace
Composer & Sound Designer Philip Stewart
Movement Director Paula O'Reilly
Voice Director Andrea Ainsworth
Casting Director Sarah Jones
Production Dramaturg Tanya Dean
Hair & Makeup Designer Leonard Daly
Associate Composer & Sound Designer Jane Deasy
Assistant Lighting Designer Matt Burke
Publicity Image Finn Richards

Characters

The Family

Orgon
son of Madame Pernelle, husband of Elmire,
father of Mariane and Damis

Madame Pernelle
Orgon's mother

Elmire
Orgon's second wife, Mariane and Damis's stepmother

Mariane
Orgon's daughter

Damis
Orgon's son

Cleante
Elmire's brother, Orgon's brother-in-law

Tartuffe
the imposter

Dorine
Mariane's maid

Valere
Mariane's suitor

Filipote
Madame Pernelle's maid

Monsieur Loyal

Arresting Officer

TARTUFFE

Act One

Pernelle, Elmire, Dorine, Damis, Mariane, Cleante, Filipote.

Pernelle
Waste no more of my time – get me my coat.

Elmire
Hold your horses – my heart's coming up my throat.

Pernelle
No need to bother showing me the door.
You've done your duty – none could have done more.

Elmire
We're happy to show all that's due to you.
Ma belle mère, why the haste? This hullabaloo –

Pernelle
This house, all in it, put them to the sword –
Morning, noon and night no one heeds a word,
Respect for all has gone out the window.
A madhouse, bedlam – time that I go.

Dorine
If I may –

Pernelle
You may not, you're a servant,
Too full of your own voice – you will, you won't,
You'll this, you'll that, you think you know it all.

Damis
But – but –

Pernelle
Young man, you're heading for a fall,
I warn you of that, your own grandmother.

I told my son you'd only cause bother,
Showing you're bad news at every chance,
Leading all to hell in your merry dance.

Mariane
I think –

Pernelle
Oh the sister, the quiet one,
As she pretends, playing ever so dumb,
Would butter or cheese melt inside your mouth,
Too sweet to be wholesome, rarely strayed from Louth?
Still waters run deep, no truer word spoken,
You're up to badness in ways well hidden.

Elmire
But Mother –

Pernelle
Don't bother me, daughter-in-law.
I find you, my lady, the right hard chaw.
Set them good example, these wayward brats.
Their mother who died, she knew what was what.
You spend money like it grows on the trees.
Strutting peahen, you should be on your knees.
See fit to delight the husband you've wed.
Show the pound of flesh in the marriage bed.

Cleante
Madame, please –

Pernelle
If I were my son, that woman's good spouse,
I fear I would have you barred from this house.
You put into practice just what you preach,
I do not admire the laxness you teach,
Nor could a decent, clean-living Christian.
I speak as I find and I fear no man.
I don't mince my words when my gander's raised.

Damis

And Monsieur Tartuffe grows fat on your praise.

Pernelle

The man is blessed – no shadow of doubt.
A paragon – not a lump of a lout,
Such as yourself who's only out to mock.

Damis

So I've to treasure this diamond, this rock?
He saunters in here, his wish our command –
He tells us to sit and he tells us to stand.
We do as he bids, master of no revels,
Or else we will end up burning in hell?
Nothing escapes his ever eagle eye –
One single slip, you're hung out to dry.

Pernelle

Is it not right and proper he should be so?
Only one place that upright man will go –
Heaven, that's why my son should be his match,
And keep the lot of you under severe latch.

Damis

I'd defy any father on this earth
To allow that scoundrel the slightest worth.
Give me a chance and I swear I'll not miss,
Let me flatten that peasant with either fist.

Dorine

If you ask me, it is beyond scandal
A stranger now rules within these four walls,
A beggar arrived not a shoe on his foot,
You could see the moon in the shine of his suit,
Now he's getting somewhat carried away,
Thinking he's the master and he holds sway.

Pernelle

Mother of the divine crucified saviour,
May we all bask in that pious man's fervour.

Dorine

You have him canonised a living saint –
Tar and feather him, smear whitewash and paint,
Too good for the chancer –

Pernelle

Watch your tongue –

Dorine

God speed the day I see him hung.

Pernelle

Tartuffe is goodness, goodness incarnate –
I swear on my soul, turn aside from hate,
All you who reject him and wish him ill.
Listen to me, swallow this bitter pill.
What does he do but tell a few home truths?
Sin and sin alone provokes him to wrath.
He bears on his back the mark of heaven.

Dorine

Why does he bar the door to kith and kin?
Why is it now out of bounds to visit?
That's a rule he follows like Holy Writ.
Do I need spell out what it is I mean?
Madame, he's the cat – you are the cream.

Pernelle

Be quiet, think about what you're saying.
This ceilidhing, it's not quite the done thing.
An open house is not a holy place,
Swarms gathered inside all stuffing their face,
Hanging outside the door, up to no good.
I'd like to think the best, indeed I should,
But tongues are wagging – that's not a good sign.

Cleante

Then would you have us silent for all time?
Do you think you can prevent people talking?
No, we must gossip as caged birds must sing.

Best ignore this foolish tittle-tattle.
Do your best to conduct yourself well.

Dorine

Daphne next door, the squirt she calls her man,
Might it be that pair who's taking a hand,
Spitting bile into poison pen letters,
Speaking ill of their elders and betters?
Why is it ones should be locked in a home
Are always the first to be firing stones?
The first sign they spot of something awry,
They leap on it, smelling fresh fish to fry.
They'll make sure the stars in the heaven know
Who's doing what to whom down here below.
Time then to join in a chorus of blame,
Safe now to pillory whoever's shamed.

Pernelle

Same Daphne, each day what's her first and last breath?
Prayers that God grant her a happy death,
A woman to cherish, honour, revere –
She'd take a hatchet to ones flocking here,
Distracting her orisons morning, noon, night.

Dorine

Excellent, long may she shine her bright light.
No doubt she's as honest as she is austere.
Ageing has helped to make her more sincere.
Fair to say Daphne ain't the draw she was,
So she's rewriting the get-out-of-jail clause,
Since she let the squirt be her only guide,
Her piety takes the place of her pride.
She enjoyed courting once upon a time,
She now advises dips in quicklime,
Better for the soul if not the body,
Since hers has, shall we say, seen better days.
That's the way the world works, sad to observe.
Losing your looks, it's like losing your nerve –

When fellas no more gather round your flame,
They sneer in your face, take your name in vain –
What's left to do but turn into a prude,
Righteous and strict, eschewing what's rude,
Crude, rough and ready, fresh bread and wine,
Such filthy fodder, they prefer to decline.
They see fit to find fault with all they choose –
All reputations they batter and bruise,
And why? Is it for the sake of goodness?
Dignity, virtue? They couldn't care less.

Pernelle

Stuff and nonsense, nothing but fairy tales.
Daughter-in-law, no hope that sense prevails –
No chance of getting a word in edgewise,
In this house we are all cut down to size
By madam here – I christen the upstart.
She'd have us hauled before her horse and cart.
Half a chance, she'll make us all her skivvy.
Smartest thing happened to Orgon, that day
My son welcomed Tartuffe into his home.
I feel it in my waters and bones
He's come amongst you in your hour of need.
Tartuffe is a walking Apostle's Creed.
Listen to him and learn of salvation,
What roads lead to the Lord, which ways to shun.
Visits and balls, cavorting in corners,
They're not the work of Little Jack Horner –
The devil himself, Beelzebub, Satan,
There's where you spot him with his lethal clan,
No chance of a sacrament doing the rounds,
The holy Eucharist, it's spat on the ground,
The dirty chat that could turn your stomach –
That's fare for all in the land of great craic.
Songs to make a sailor blush, putrid jokes.
What is to become of clean-living folk?
Confused by the chaos and the blather,

Changeable as tomorrow's weather,
Who knows what way the wind and the rain blow?
Everybody butts in with what they know –
Listen to all this rabble's carry-on –
You could be in Babel or Babylon.
One time a doctor of theology,
He passed this bit of wisdom on to me –

She points to Cleante.

Look at the sneering puss on that fellow,
Laughing at me like a busted bellows.
You go on jeering, I've nothing to say,
I've lost my respect for you all this day.
Before I set foot in this house again,
You'll have neither curtains nor window panes.
I'll remove myself from scandalous chat.
Bad cess on the lot of you – I mean that.

She gives her servant maid Filipote a smack.

You – stop standing there, gaping and dreaming.
I know you were likely in on the scheming.
I'll warm your ear, girl, I'll tan your hide.
Move – are you waiting to be someone's bride?

Exit Pernelle, Filipote, Elmire, Mariane.

Cleante
I think I might stay put – that old lady –

Dorine
Just as well she mounts her high horse today –
She's upped and gone before you called her old.
She'd box your ears daring to be so bold.
She imagines she's still a spring chicken.

Cleante
She's more like a brooding mother hen,
Fretting over Tartuffe, her pride and joy.

Dorine
She's restraint itself compared to her boy.
Set eyes on Orgon, you'd see a basket case –
Since meeting Tartuffe master walks in a daze –
A man worth having on your side one time,
Defending the King and his noble line.
He believes that upstart like a brother,
Worships him above wife, child or mother.
They've no secrets between the pair of them.
Tartuffe alone can touch the master's hem.
He is the source of all the world's wisdom,
Pampered and coddled, his darling diddums,
Tartuffe, adored more than any sweetheart,
Cupid himself is running out of darts.
At dinner who's perched on the seat of honour?
Who else but that mouth eats enough for four?
He has first choice of all dainty morsels,
If he farts, they smell sweet as caramel.
He'll sneeze and God-bless-you drowns our ears,
The apple of the boss's eye, his hero.
He can quote from all their conversations,
You'd think that all the blaggard's said and done
Should be classed as some sort of miracle –
Hear ye, hear ye, obey the oracle.
Tartuffe, he knows which side his bread's buttered.
He knows how to set eyes all aflutter,
Cadging money through the night till morning –
Yet he dares to issue dire warnings.
He thundered in here, his eyes out on pins,
Ripped our ribbons, dumped our rouge in the bins.
Something lacy lurked in a *Lives of the Saints*,
The squeals out of him, was he going to faint?
He claims we've begun to give our blessings
On what he would call the devil's playthings.

Elmire returns.

Elmire

Lucky you let me see her to the door,
You're spared the tirade – all she's said before.
I see my husband, he's not spotted me,
I'm going upstairs – let him know I'm free.

Cleante

Courage, sister, we'll never say die.
I'll wait for him here – say hello and goodbye.

Damis

Have a word with him about my sister.
Her marriage brings Tartuffe out in blisters.
He will do all he can to delay
When my father shall name her happy day.

Dorine

Here he comes –

Exit Damis, Elmire.
  Enter Orgon.

Orgon

My dearest brother, hello.

Cleante

You just arrived, me about to go.
The countryside, not much in bloom, I hear.

Orgon

Wait, good brother-in-law, I want you near.

He turns to Dorine.

Let me know what's happening in this place.
Nothing to shame us or bring down disgrace?

Dorine

Poor Madame, her head was splitting in two,
Her temperature hit the roof, a bad flu.

Orgon
And Tartuffe?

Dorine
     Tartuffe? Always bright, never hazy,
Hale and hearty, as fresh as a daisy.

Orgon
The poor soul –

Dorine
     Could not touch a bite all day –
Breakfast, dinner, her evening supper,
Her head opening – that woman suffers.

Orgon
And Tartuffe?

Dorine
    Tartuffe?

Orgon
     My own poor Tartuffe?

Dorine
He managed to wolf a pair of partridge
As solemn as if he was taking the pledge,
Then a snack, a half-leg of mutton, minced.

Orgon
The poor man!

Dorine
    You're not great picking up hints.
Your woman never got a wink of sleep.
Burning inside, too demented to weep –
We had to stay beside her till daybreak.

Orgon
And Tartuffe?

Dorine

                  Felt a slight twinge in his neck.
Nothing a little snoozy-poo might cure –
He's out like a light, so banish all care.

Orgon

The poor man!

Dorine

                  Madame let herself be bled –
Roaring like a bull, the sheets turning red –
After all that, she felt as right as rain.

Orgon

And Tartuffe?

Dorine

                  Tartuffe could endure her pain.
To make up for the blood my sweet lady lost
He downed a dose of wine for his breakfast.
I will let Madame know your deep concern.
We can hope for the best – she'll live and learn.

Exit Dorine.

Cleante

She's laughing at you in front of your face.
Far be it from me to put her in her place,
But I will say to you she has good reason.
Who under God can explain what's going on?
In this day and age, what magic's afloat
That such a creature grabs you by the throat?
You abandon us all for his damned sake.
Do you not see with him it's take, take, take?
Inside your home his pockets grow heavy –
It's got to the stage –

Orgon

                  Brother, let it be,
You don't know the man you're talking about.

Cleante

I know next to nothing but that he's a lout,
So it's not hard to see he's a dead loss –

Orgon

You could be charmed should your paths ever cross.
Spellbound, I'd say, eating out of his hand –
He is a man – this Tartuffe – what a man!
He points the way to redemption and peace.
What the world values most he values least.
I am a changed man when he talks to me,
His good works and words alone set us free.
I obey precisely his every wish,
Even if mother, wife, children perish –
That would not trouble me in the slightest.
He is quite simply my absolute best –

Cleante

What a family man! Aren't you a credit?

Orgon

Would you'd set eyes on him when we first met –
You'd feel for him everything that I do.
In church each morning – I swear this is true –
That gentle man would kneel opposite me,
Looking heavenwards, down on his bended knees,
Praying with a passion all could witness,
Offering the Lord his most fervent kiss.
As if he could give me the moon and stars,
He drenched me, leaving, in holy water.
I learned from his servant – a match the pair –
They were living on nothing but fresh air.
I gave him alms – the man gave half back,
It's too much, he said, more than me are lacking.
When I refused, before my very eyes,
The poor got the lot – no word of a lie.
Heaven itself made him my honoured guest.
All seems to be working out for the best.

He misses nothing when it comes to my good name.
As for my wife, he takes infinite pains
To warn me if men stray out of order.
Always one eye cast over his shoulder,
He's six times more possessive than I'd be,
He sees things I've never managed to see.
He is as severe as he is sincere,
One step out of line and you will soon hear.
The smallest slip-up, he's scarlet with shame,
And always but always, himself he blames.
Like the other day, saying Hail Marys,
A dirty big flea, stinking and hairy,
Bit him – he squashed it into tiny pieces,
Then cried aloud, forgive me, Jesus.

Cleante

Brother, good God, have you gone quite insane?
You mock me, don't you, chanting this refrain?

Orgon

And I'm in no mood for taking your lip.
It strikes me as worse than devil worship.
I have no time with your impious ilk,
Drunk as a skunk on Satan's buttermilk.
If I've warned you once, for the thousandth time,
God's law means the punishment fits the crime.

Cleante

I know what I'm saying – heaven knows my heart.
I'll have no truck with the hypocrite's art.
The brave and the good have no need to brag.
They say nothing till the game's in the bag.
They get the job done, without favours asked.
God gave them a face not needing a mask.
Try not to confuse the real with the dud.
First sign of lying, nip it in the bud.
Man is a mad, insatiable animal.
We go beyond the beyonds without fail.

I know how to tell the false from the true.
Good men, above all, I've come to value.
All busy bodies I hate and despise,
Poison on their tongues, spite in their eyes.
Charlatans letting on they're the best in the land,
They'd knife you as soon as stretch out their hands.
All they want is promotion and credit.
They fawn on false friends with little merit.
They claim they are the army of the Lord,
Brandishing His divine, righteous sword.
That's what they'd employ to strike us all down,
But spare themselves seeing God's vengeful frown.
He knows how to sort the wheat from the chaff,
He knows who deserves the fatted calf.
I don't dispute some are truly devout,
Genuine, gracious, doing without –
They are not devoured alive with disdain,
And if I so choose, I could name their names.
Their faith is humane and benevolent.
They believe in love that is heaven-sent.
All they're trying to do, it's to live well.
To be blunt, these are my sort of people.
You raise Tartuffe above all you admire.
The sun's in your eyes, beware of fire.

Orgon

Have you finished?

Cleante

Yes.

Orgon

I'll beg to differ.
Any other advice? What to eat for dinner?

Cleante

Valere, Mariane, about their wedding,
You promised the lad –

26

Orgon

Do I need reminding?

Cleante
You'd settled a date when they could marry –

Orgon
True.

Cleante

Why have you decided to delay –

Orgon
Don't know.

Cleante

Could it be you're entertaining –

Orgon
Could be.

Cleante

Rule out hope for any ring?

Orgon
I'm not saying that –

Cleante

Why be so wily?
Answer me – yes or no, what's it to be?
What can prevent you keeping your promise?
There's nothing –

Orgon

This and that and that and this –

Cleante
Valere asked me to talk –

Orgon

May God be praised.

Cleante
What will I tell him?

Orgon

Do nothing in haste.

Cleante
Tell me your plans and stop this merry dance.

Orgon
I plan to do whatever heaven wants.

Cleante
Will you keep your promise to Valere?
Why would you break your word – why would you dare?

He sees Orgon has left.

Unfortunate boy, most unhappy pair,
I must warn them misfortune's in the air.

Exit Cleante.

Act Two

Enter Mariane.

Orgon
Mariane?

Mariane
       Father?

Orgon
            In private, my pearl.

Orgon is looking into a closet.

Mariane
What are you looking for?

Orgon
               Know this, girl –
These walls have ears, anyone could listen.
This house is perfect for spies to find dens.
Mariane, I admire your gentleness.
Of all my family, I love you best.

Mariane
I am obliged to Father's loving care –

Orgon
Well said, my daughter, but now you must swear,
Your only concern must be to please me.

Mariane
I pride myself that is how things should be.

Orgon
Good – what do you make of Tartuffe, our guest?

29

Mariane
    Me?

Orgon
        You – this is my special request –

Mariane
    I'll say whatever you want about him.

Orgon
    Wisely spoken – no nonsense nor whims.
    Tell me a light shines out of his person.
    You'll give him your heart he's already won.
    You'll do as I want – make him your husband.

Mariane moves back in surprise.

Mariane
    What?

Orgon
        Something's up?

Mariane
                I don't understand –

Orgon
    What?

Mariane
        I don't follow –

Orgon
                What –

Mariane
                    What Father wants.
    What light, what husband, where is this romance –

Orgon
    Tartuffe –

Mariane

Not so – never so – I'd rather die –
Why make me confess to the worst of lies?

Orgon

I want it so – I want it to be true,
That is my decree, that is what you'll do.
Tartuffe will become my flesh and my blood
When he marries you by the grace of God –
Your legal husband, till death doth us part,
Loyal, loving –

He sees Dorine.

What do you want to start?
What do they say about curious cats?
They come to sad ends – remember that.

Dorine

Is it a rumour – am I just hearing things –
A flight to the moon on gossamer wings?
Who's the lunatic raving and roaring?
What's the buzz about this wedding story?

Orgon

Why do you find it so hard to believe?

Dorine

You really expect me to be that naïve –

Orgon

It's going to happen, like it or lump –

Dorine

Away with you, I'll start taking the hump.

Orgon

I warn you, sooner rather than later –

Dorine

Nonsense –

Orgon
                         Daughter, it's no laughing matter.

Dorine
  He's joking, your father, the great big cod.

Orgon
  I'm telling you –

Dorine
                         Between a wink and nod.

Orgon
  It shall erupt, my most righteous ire.

Dorine
  Do, and I'll pull up my chair to the fire.
  You look like a man of immense good sense –
  I adore your moustache all jungly and dense.
  Are you bonkers enough –

Orgon
                              You hold it right there.
  You shoot off your mouth every nook and cranny –
  I can take no more, you get on my –

Dorine
  Violets, sweet violets, please.
  You must be pulling our leg with this scheme.
  You'll fulfil the hypocrite's hopes and dreams.
  Tell him to keep his claws off your daughter.
  Prove to us blood is thicker than water.
  How would you benefit from this union?
  You're a wealthy man, and Tartuffe is scum.
  Why choose a beggar –

Orgon
                         Quiet – he has nothing,
  That's why I revere the man so highly,
  I honour his proud, simple poverty.
  He turns his back on plenty and profit,

The spirit moves through him, God love his wit.
The man has lost all he once did possess.
How does he react? Always with God-bless.
I will help him recover all his lands –
His home estates that should be back in his hands.
See for yourself – he is a gentleman.

Dorine
Quite so, the paragon – putrid and vain.
You're going to hand over Mariane,
A girl, a good girl, tell me how you can?
So she will become his goods and chattels –
Why not just leave her at the gates of hell?
In the name of what's decent, think again.
What can come of this but heartache and pain?
You can destroy a young woman's virtue.
Don't force her to do what she cannot do.
What's the first rule being happy together?
To give and take through foul and fair weather.
You know who puts horns on a husband's head?
Himself, who drove her from the marriage bed.
Some men do not deserve their wedding vows.
Be loyal to such brutes? Just tell me how!
Give your daughter to one she detests –
Ruination follows, you know the rest.

Orgon turns to Mariane.

Orgon
Now she writes the rules, chapter and verse.

Dorine
I give my advice, you could follow worse.

Orgon
I'll waste no time, daughter, with this blather.
I know what's good for you, I'm your father.
I'd given Valere my word in this matter.
But the boy gambles money like water.

I suspect he's no time for priest or nun.
His prayers and Aves are quickly done.

Dorine
You'd like him to be there at your beck and call,
There to be noticed where your shadow falls,
Wrapping rosaries around his fingers.

Orgon
When I need it, I'll ask for your answer.

Dorine
I speak out in your own good interest.

Orgon
I think I can decide what's for the best.

Dorine
If we did not love you –

Orgon
                                        Your love be stuffed –

Dorine
No, I'll keep on – I will not be put off –

Orgon
Once and for all, will you shut it, you snake?

Dorine
Hitched to that hallion, I'd break my own neck.

Orgon
Do you ignore what I tell you to do?

Dorine
You're whinging – why? I'm not talking to you.

Orgon
Then who could it be you deign to address?

Dorine
I talk to myself – isn't that for the best?

Orgon places himself in a position to slap Dorine.

Orgon
Why do you muddle whatever I plan?

*Whenever he looks at Dorine, she stands bolt upright,
without speaking.*

I'll have to show you the back of my hand.

Dorine remains silent.

What has now stopped you contradicting me?

Dorine
Nothing to report but fiddle-de-dee.

Orgon
Go on, one word more –

Dorine
                              No – not in the mood.

Orgon
Daughter, you must do as you know you should.
Obey and respect what I choose for you.

Dorine
Tie her to him, you'd need stronger than glue.

*Orgon goes to give her a slap, but he misses, and she's
gone.*

Orgon
That girl has my heart scalded completely –
Live with her longer, you might well agree
She'll drive me to doing something sinful.
She has me panting like a dangerous bull –
Such cheek, such impudence, it's unhinged my mind.
I need a walk, leave these ructions behind –

Exit Orgon.

Dorine

Has the cat got your tongue, Miss Mariane?
Is it up to me to foil this mad plan?
You say nothing – are you in on the act?
Don't you agree that it's insane, this pact?

Mariane

What should I do when Father's a tyrant?

Dorine

You do what needs doing to get what you want.
If Tartuffe is such a wonderful catch,
Your father and him make the perfect match.
Now look – Valere, do you love him or not?

Mariane

You do me wrong – his love is all I've got.

Dorine

You do then –

Mariane

Adore him with all my life –

Dorine

He will do anything to make you his wife.
And you are as keen, burning with desire?

Mariane

Absolutely –

Dorine

How do we dump the liar?

Mariane

I'll kill myself if I'm forced to take him.

Dorine

Brilliant – clever, let's go out on that limb.
All you need to do is to drop down dead.
Was that the first thing to enter your head?
A super-duper, wicked solution.

Why did I not think that's what should be done?
Maybe because it's just plain bloody daft.
I ask have you a titter of wit left?

Mariane
What do you want of me?

Dorine
Nothing – nothing.
I hear now a little bell ring-a-ding-dinging –
Guess what it tells me? Hosannas be sung,
Joy unconfined for the old and the young!
Take up this offer, you've found your fella.
Is he not divine? Is he not just swell?
Why not give the world and his wife a laugh?
What great good fortune – be his other half.
In his part of the world he's the bee's knees.
Bow down, obey – watch him do as he'd please.
A prince among men, face like a beetroot.
What good living lass would give him the boot?

Mariane
Just get me out of this – you win hands down.

Dorine
I could not risk your severe father's frown.
A daughter should obey her kith and kin.
So, she marries a monkey – that's no sin.
Your choice – tell me, why are you complaining?
Enjoy all the comforts this connection brings.
The magistrate's missus – the tax collector –
Uncles in droves, here are your new neighbours.
They'll welcome you warmly with open arms,
The middle of nowhere, but what harm?
Have a smashing time, come carnival –
Two bagpipes, some puppets, the haymakers' ball.
Your future with him –

37

Mariane

                    You are killing me.
Think instead of some way to set me free.
You've been loyal to me, beyond reproof –

Dorine

And now, you are going to be Tarfuffed.
You'll soon get a severe whiff of that lad –

Mariane

My heart is breaking, and you – you are glad.
You dance on my sorrow and my despair.
If I should live or die what do I care?
There's only one cure for what torments me –

She goes to leave.

Dorine

Come back to me, I've stopped being angry.
Yes, indeed, you deserve all my pity.

Mariane

I tell you, Dorine, I know how to die.
Father tortures me – can you tell me why?

Dorine

Rest yourself, we'll find a way forward –
Right on the button, ferocious and hard,
Here comes your Valere –

Enter Valere.

Valere

                    This is some shock,
This bit of news, is it me who's the mock?

Mariane

He's coming up with this, himself, my father –

Valere

Are you serious?

Mariane

Yes, I am – I swear –
He's changed his mind –

Valere

So where then do you stand?

Mariane

I don't know – if his wish is my command –

Valere

You don't know – nice –

Mariane

What's your advice for me –

Valere

.. take that man for your husband – marry.

Mariane

Very well – I'll do as you say exactly.

Valere

Do so, Madame, if that makes you content.

Mariane

Thank you kindly, aren't you heaven-sent?

Dorine (*aside*)

See what comes of this –

Valere

So I was deceived?
You said, here's my heart, and you were believed.
There was no truth in the love you declared?
When it comes to women, men must beware.
You know what I say? I say right you be.
A flotilla of fish swim in the sea.
I know one smasher, she's head over heels –
Cracked about me – that's what she feels.

Mariane
I'm so glad to learn you will recover.
Have a whale of a time with this – lover.

Valere
Is that what you wish?

Mariane
                    You've got it in one.

Valere
I'm out the door, goodbye and I'm gone.
Never forget who made sure that must be.
This is the last time you'll ever see me.

Mariane
No loss.

Near the door Valere stops.

Valere
        Yes?

Mariane
                What?

Valere
                        Is that you calling?

Mariane
Me? You're dreaming –

Valere
                        Forgive me stalling.
Adieu, Madame –

Mariane
                Adieu, sir –

Dorine
                        Call it quits.
I've had my fill of this, put down your mitts.

*She goes to Valere to stop him by the arm. He pretends
to resist strongly.*

Valere

Dorine, what do you want?

Dorine

                You both, come here.
He loves you, you love him – that much is clear.

They do so.

Valere

Don't look as if I've just crawled from the sink.
Give a man a chance – or even a wink.

*Mariane turns her eyes to Valere and gives him a little
smile.*

Dorine

Young ones in love – welcome home to bedlam.
Faults on both sides, cut out the high drama.
Might I suggest we pull the finger out?
Any thoughts how we put this Tartuffe to rout?

They shake their heads.

Act the innocent, do all you are told.
Let your father think you're as good as gold.
If he still insists on spilling the salt –
Then you can call these proceedings to a halt.
Invent some illness that has laid you low,
Its symptoms demand you must take things slow.
Another time say you broke a mirror,
You dreamt of the dead, or muddy water.
Look, above all else, this I do declare –
Who will you choose to marry? It's Valere.
Best though you're not found acting in cahoots –
That way we'll keep Tartuffe's paws off the loot.
Don't be seen even talking together.
Now, gather your friends true or fairweather.

They'll help you get what you have been promised.
The brother and granny, they're on my list –
Be off –

Valere goes to speak, bowing and scraping.

      Do me a favour – cease yapping.
Sicken a goat, this bowing and scraping.
You go this way, you can go the other.
Morning, noon and night, nothing but bother.

Exit Valere and Mariane.

Act Three

Dorine

    Here he comes, Damis, son and the heir,
    Fit to be tied, barging in like a bear.

Enter Damis.

Damis

    May heaven itself beat me black and blue,
    If I let another tell me what to do.
    Call me what you like – coward and gutless –
    Should I not put a quick stop to this mess.

Dorine

    Your father, we will soon soften his cough,
    Himself was only shooting his mouth off.
    The world does not work according to his whim.
    There are ways and means of defying him.

Damis

    I would like a quiet word in his ear –

Dorine

    Leave this to your stepmother – never fear,
    She can handle Tartuffe and your papa.
    She knows the ins and outs of this saga.
    She has the hypocrite round her finger.
    One smile, that lad's away in a manger.
    Tartuffe sweet on her would be a fine thing!
    You know why she might be pulling his strings?
    It could come down to our best interests.
    Is he determined to feather his nest?
    He must be left alone saying his prayers,
    But I'm told he will soon descend the stairs.
    I'll talk with him – will you make your exit?

Damis

I would love a quick word, just let me sit –

Dorine

I will not – we need to be left on our own.

Damis

I won't get annoyed, silent as a stone –

Dorine points to his mouth.

Dorine

A mouth like a gateway that's never shut,
You'll ruin everything – no more ifs nor buts.
Out of my sight now – look, here's him coming.

Enter Tartuffe.
   Damis hides, but Tartuffe does catch sight of Dorine.

Tartuffe

My scourge and my hair-shirt, put them away.
I pray that heaven protects you this day.
I go to the prison to share my alms,
Felons are also the Lord's little lambs.

Dorine

I think my stomach will soon be quite sick.
If I listen more to this pretentious – violets, sweet violets.

Tartuffe

What is it you want?

Dorine

                    I've asked you to come –

Tartuffe takes a handkerchief from his pocket.

Tartuffe

Take this handkerchief, cover your bosoms.
Nakedness lures all men to their damnation.
Such sights have unmanned an army of souls.
Sin can possess us when we lose control.

Dorine

    You're that easy prey to all temptation?
    A flash of flesh, and thy kingdom comes?
    I must say you have me rightly flummoxed.
    What lad or lassie would water your rocks?
    Maybe you reside in ivory towers.
    I could strip you of your hairy drawers,
    I would not peep at your willy winkle –
    That's the God's truth, I'd swear on your bible.

Tartuffe

    Pray try to curb such foul, immodest talk.
    One word more like that, I warn you I'll walk.

Dorine

    Madame, she wants a word, would you oblige?

Tartuffe

    Of course –

Dorine (*aside*)

    Her knight consort, her loving liege,
    I tell you I've read this just like a book –

Tartuffe

    Will she be down soon?

Dorine

                      Why not have a look?

Exit Dorine.
   Enter Elmire.

Tartuffe

    May heaven bless you, both soul and body,
    May those touched by love stand always ready
    To wish you may thrive in excellent health
    And enjoy abundance of worldly wealth.

Elmire

    I am most grateful, these wishes are pious,
    Sit here at our ease and forget about fuss.

Tartuffe

You feel better after your malady?

Elmire

Much better – the fever passed quite quickly.

Tartuffe

I say my prayers, I beg of the Lord,
Do unto us according to Thy Word,
That way it will stop, whatever ails you.
You'll be right as rain in a day or two.

Elmire

It's fair to say your concern is excessive.

Tartuffe

We choose how to die, we choose how to live –
I'd give you my good health, were it up to me –

Elmire

That goes well beyond Christian charity.
For such mercy, I am deep in your debt.

Tartuffe

I could do even more, were you to let –

Elmire

There is one matter I'd like to discuss,
Right now in private, just the two of us.

Tartuffe

Then I'm so happy we are of one mind,
I'll tell you straight, were I deaf, dumb and blind,
This is what I'd implore, above all cures,
God grants me great favour, you can be sure.

Elmire

I merely ask for a quick word or two –
Be honest with me, speak only what's true.

Tartuffe

I would strip my soul bare before your eyes –
I swear there was not a trace of a lie
When I censured your gentleman callers,
Arriving en masse and smelling your hair,
Touching your soft hand and kissing your cheek,
Abusing your good self, so gentle and meek.
My harsh words, they were all for your own good,
I ask only you behave as you should.
Madame, my motive could not be purer –

Elmire

I thought that myself – are we not a pair,
One addicted to the other's salvation?

Tartuffe squeezes the tips of her fingers.

Tartuffe

I think you know where it is my thoughts run.
I blaze and I burn under my hair-shirt,
With such fervour and zeal –

Elmire

                    Stop – that hurts.

He puts his hand on her knee.

What's your hand doing?

Tartuffe

Toing and froing, froing and toing.
Your dress, it's so soft – wonderful fabric.

Elmire

Stop – I have tickles, I'll scream myself sick.

She moves her chair back and Tartuffe moves his nearer.

Tartuffe

Let me look at this lace, its workmanship.
The tiniest tear, these stitches would rip,
Most delicate dress that's ever been made.

Elmire

I wish to talk, sir, I will not be nayed.
My husband would wed his daughter to you.
He will break his word, can such things be true?

Tartuffe

I heard that mentioned, only in passing,
But that's not what would make my poor heart sing.
No, I plan to bring big smiles to my face,
By looking elsewhere – can you guess what place?
That's where I'll fulfil my special desires –
Not angel nor saint but transcending higher –

Elmire

Something more rare than mere country matters?

Tartuffe

I'm not cut from stone – wound me, I shatter.

Elmire

I hear your sighs to the heavens above.
The world of the spirit, that's what you love.

Tartuffe

God created all physical beauty.
Worshipping it is our moral duty.
What's perfect passeth all comprehension.
We must submit to love in the long run.
Madame, there are miracles in your face.
Your eyes move my heart, they leave me dazed.
I see you, most excellent of creatures,
You are the bait, the quarry and the lure
That God Himself – of this I am quite sure –
Will attract all that do His sacred will.
In you I've seen His goodness, and do still.
For a time I feared how reckless I'd grown,
Me a sad sack of worthless blood and bone.
Evil spirits might cast me in their spell,
Ravenous and raging, the hounds of hell.
I must abandon you – avoid and shun

48

All you'd do to rob me of redemption –
But this cannot be a guilty passion.
I speak now with modesty and virtue,
I dare offer my guileless heart to you.
I am so bold to hope you will receive
My hand, my hope, my health – do not be grieved.
A man, a most unworthy speck of dust,
Expects you will do as he begs you must.
Give me your answer, what is it to be?
Decide, am I miserable or happy?

Elmire

How gallant indeed, this declaration,
But I admit you leave me standing stunned.
Better you steeled your heart, showed caution,
And questioned is this the best solution,
For a man like yourself, devout as a dove –

Tartuffe

Devout, yes – but I am still a man in love,
And you are divine, so my reason fails.
Madame, I am neither saint nor angel.
Do you blame me making this confession?
So I ask you, give me this concession –
Admit your blame, for being so lovely –
Enchantress, I pray you, set me free.
There is something in you more than mortal,
Something uncanny, like a crystal ball.
I tried to resist, fasting, prayers, tears –
To no point, I saw nothing but my dear.
I sobbed and I sighed, hoping you'd hear me,
I longed for you, but it was not to be,
Till now when my words explain my ardour.
Treat me most gently, don't show me the door.
I am the unworthiest of all slaves,
Chastise me, beat me, send me to the grave.
Bark what you demand, I'll always obey.
I won't breathe a word of what happened this day.

I am not one of those bragging blaggards
Can't wait to bellow through the courtyard
Favours received and progress reported,
Spilling the secrets from fond lovers' beds.
People like us, we're the soul of discretion.
We'd do the opposite, we can keep mum.
Do me this honour, all will turn out well,
Pleasure without fear, love without scandal.

Elmire

I hear you explain with such eloquence
What I'm to do in this merry dance.
Are you not worried I'll tell my husband?
You'd risk expulsion from the Promised Land?

Tartuffe

You are too benevolent to do that.
I've learned a few things from our little chats.
This is my weakness, and you sympathise,
I act on the evidence of my eyes –
What can a man do with blood in his veins?
You have all the power, you control the reins.

Elmire

Others might differ from that opinion,
But you're right, we need to show discretion.
I'll be silent as your average sphinx,
I won't breathe a word about your high jinks,
You will support what we had all planned,
The marriage of Valere and Mariane.
Let this be the end of your best efforts
To profit from another's pain and hurt.

Damis comes out from where he has hidden.

Damis

No, Madame, speak out – this I must insist,
I heard everything, how could I miss?
Heaven itself led me to this traitor,
I will flatten him on this very floor,

For his pride and malice in harming me.
I'll crush his arrogant hypocrisy.
I will show my father in broad daylight
This abomination in the Lord's sight –

Elmire

No, Damis, it's enough he'll change his ways.
I've promised him pardon – do as I say.
It's not in my nature to go and whinge.
He's a reeking big fool, his goods are singed.
A woman laughs at such shenanigans –
She'll handle herself a ludicrous man.

Damis

You have your good reasons and I have mine.
You'd spare that joke, that waste of space and time?
He has pushed me beyond provocation.
He's warped the bond between father and son.
He has caused mayhem here inside our home –
I'd crack him as I would a chicken bone.
At Valere and myself he's spit poison.
My father needs to know what's going on –
The truth about this most treacherous wretch,
This filthy-minded, scabrous, dirty letch.
Here is a God-given opportunity
To root him out of here nice and easy.
I have to grab this chance of a lifetime.
Letting him off would be a bloody crime.

Elmire

Damn –

Damis

        I have to trust myself and take my chance.
Don't try to talk me out of this vengeance.
I want this wrapped up with no more ado.
What's my first step? Well, I'll give you this clue –

Orgon appears.

We greet you, Father, with much good tidings,
I'll tell them and I hope your heart takes wing.
This gentleman, you've heard all he's professed,
His love for you – respect for your goodness –
Then why does he show you such dishonour?
Why would he be your wife's paramour?
I've heard him declare guilty devotion –
She forgave him after all he's done.
Her discreet heart wants us to say nothing,
But I say get him, make the blighter swing.

Elmire

These bullish words, to me they ring hollow.
Who'd want as a rival this gigolo?
A man plagues a woman – thinking she's meek –
Knock him into the middle of next week.
That's my advice – what I would surely do.
You'd follow that, if I'd influenced you.

Exit Elmire.

Orgon

God above, can I credit what's been said?

Tartuffe

Yes, brother, pour the shame upon my head –
A sinner sour with his iniquity,
Rotten to the core with his villainy.
Heaven bestows on me this punishment –
In God's eyes I am misshapen and bent.
He seeks to mortify me entirely.
I accept whatever is hurled at me.
Believe just what you're told, steel your anger,
Banish me from your home, let me wander,
So brand me with more than the mark of Cain,
Burden me with disgrace and all ill fame.

Orgon turns to his son.

Orgon
You worthless scoundrel, because he is pure,
You lie and tarnish him, you corrupt cur.

Damis
What? This damned hypocrite makes you deny –

Orgon
Quiet – you're accursed, I say damn your eyes.

Tartuffe
Just let him speak – you accuse him wrongly.
You'd do better to believe and be swayed.
The simple truth is that I am without worth,
Best I'm removed from the face of the earth.

Tartuffe addresses Damis.

Yes, yes, my boy, address me as traitor,
A lost soul, a thief, wretched murderer –
Shower even worse accusations on me.
I won't deny them, I see what you see.
Hammer your nails through my sinews and nerves.
I will bear the scars of all I deserve.

Orgon speaks to Tartuffe.

Orgon
Brother, too much –

Orgon speaks to Damis.

                              And you won't give in.

Damis
Has this hypocrite driven you insane?

Orgon speaks to Tartuffe.

Orgon
My brother, rise –

Damis

The waster can –

Orgon

Quiet.

Damis

Why all this growling – am I now your pet?
Do you take me for a dog in a cage?

Orgon

One word more and I will break both your legs.

Tartuffe

For the love of God, brother, just calm down.
Please see to it he remains safe and sound –
Damis must not receive the slightest scratch.
I pray he may never meet with his match.
I'll go on both knees and ask you excuse –

Orgon

Are you serious?

Orgon turns to Damis.

See how good he is!

Damis

And so?

Orgon

Silence!

Damis

What if –

Orgon

I said, silence.
I know why you go on the offensive.
You hate Tartuffe, that I can see clearly.
Wife, children, servants – you're all against me.
You want him kicked out to walk the cold streets.
You're not fit to wash the soles of his feet.

The more attempts made to have him banished,
The more I'll have him near, just as I wish.
I'll give him my daughter to be his wife.
I'll spite my own shower whose pride runs rife.

Damis

You intend forcing her to take his hand?

Orgon

Yes, you ruffian, you and your merry band,
I'll stand against you till you comprehend
I will be obeyed – let that be the end.
Face one fact, big man – I am the master.
Get down on your knees, try to pass muster,
Ask Tartuffe in his goodness to absolve –

Damis

That good-for-nothing? What might that involve?
Pretending to believe he's righteous –

Orgon

So you refuse? May you turn into dust.
A stick, give me a stick, don't hold me back.
Get out of my house with your dirty tricks.
Never dare darken my front door again.

Damis

I will leave, but –

Orgon

Get out, I won't explain
Why I disinherit you, not a sou –
I curse you as well, just so you should know.

Exit Damis.

To insult a holy man so freely –

Tartuffe

Pardon him for the wrongs he did to me.
I try to protect your reputation.
They blacken my name – cut me to the bone.

I hate such base acts of ingratitude.
They are the mark of the vulgar and lewd.
My heart breaks in two, I stand horrified –
So much that I think I'm going to die.

*In tears, Orgon runs to the door through which he
chased his son.*

Orgon

You devil, I'm sorry I spared you my hand.
I'd flatten you now, I'd leave you unmanned.

Tartuffe

Calm down, brother, don't be so angry.
These painful quarrels, let's put them aside.
I needs must find a pit where I can hide –
On the house I've brought both rancour and hate.
I need to leave sooner rather than late –

Orgon

You're not serious –

Tartuffe

Here I'm detested.
They'll turn you against me. You'll hear what's said –
Please never doubt my sincerity –

Orgon

Nothing will separate Tartuffe from me.
Do you see me attending to that pack?

Tartuffe

They will not cease stabbing me in the back.
You say you'll refuse point blank to listen,
But someday you will, it's a question when.

Orgon

Never, brother, never –

Tartuffe

Husbands are fools.
A wife can play games, he will lose his soul.

Orgon

No, no –

Tartuffe

I will be gone, you will be safe.
I give you the gift of my sinful life.
There's now no more need to attack me –

Orgon

You will stay here – that's the master's decree.
On you and you alone my life depends.

Tartuffe

I'm mortified – your wish is my command.
Friendship requires honour be kept intact.
Allow me to tell you I've never lacked
A most judicious sense of what is what –
Avoid scandal, a good name can't be bought.
I will shun your wife, and I won't see you.

Orgon

Continue to plague her – that's what we'll do.
You'll be in her company morn to night.
Annoying all hands – that's my great delight.
Wait for this – I'll leave them without a chair –
I'm going to make you my only heir.
My entire estate, bricks, mortar and straw –
The lot goes to my future son-in-law.
You mean more than wife and family.
My good and frank friend, take it all from me.

Tartuffe

May the will of God be done in all things.
He hath raised the lowly high as a king.

Orgon

Poor man – let's sign this up, that's what we'll do.
Let them burst their gut, seething in their stew.

Exit Orgon.

Act Four

Enter Cleante, Tartuffe.

Cleante

Take my word all are talking about it.
What's said does not help you one little bit.
I'm very glad to find our paths have crossed –
It's not my business what's been gained or lost,
I'll stick to the worst case scenario.
Suppose Damis let his quick temper go,
And you were indeed the injured party,
Would it not be Christian charity
To turn your heart away from vengeance?
Is that not above the shillings and the pence?
Will you allow your quarrel to dictate
A son should be barred from his father's gate?
I'll say it once more – I dare to declare
No one could approve this state of affairs.
Smooth things over, settle these ructions.
Don't urge more war between father and son.
Act the peacemaker, as God once blessed us.

Tartuffe

I'd like to oblige and play down this fuss.
I harbour resentment against no man.
Were he before me, alone, pale and wan,
I would not revel in his want and wail –
But the heavens themselves keep on my tail,
Demanding I do what is right and fair.
Should he venture back, I needs must prepare
Abandon this house and curse all within.
What he did to me was a mortal sin.
We must avoid the slightest contact.

Nothing between us – no hint of a pact
Must give rise to any talk of scandal.
Look at them turning their backs to the wall.
I hear them flying, the poisonous darts,
Saying it's pure politics on my part,
Pretending to pity my accuser,
Myself who received only his abuse.
They'd all maintain I showed a blind eye
And let him continue to poke and pry.

Cleante

Since when did God need a lynching party?
He'll deal with your like shortly and smartly,
He has no time for talk of paying back,
Since He shows, above all else, what you lack,
Forgiveness of sin, His judgement divine,
The font of all mercy, absolver of crime.
Who gives a damn what people might say
When others wrong us – who shows us the way?
We should listen and do all that God ordains.
He asks only that – it will not be in vain.

Tartuffe

Heaven decrees that I must forgive him,
It does not command that I live with him.

Cleante

Does it command not to bear false witness?
His father's heart – that you should redress –

Tartuffe

There's not a selfish bone in my body.
With that much my friends all readily agree.
Offer me earth, its kingdoms, its cities –
I'd refuse, shake my head, say how pretty.
But no – not for me, all this false glitter.
When it comes to greed, I'm quite the quitter.
Yes, I will take all Orgon hands over.
For that man there's no favour I would spare.

All that treasure must be bad temptation.
It might well spell ruination for some.
They might realise their evil designs.
Not me, I'll use it with one thought in mind –
The glory of God, and for my neighbours.
No one will be turned away from my door.

Cleante

Such delicate scruples do become you.
Leave them – the rightful heir knows what to do.
It is his to lavish and to squander,
Not your cash to squirrel or to launder.
Your brass neck in this business quite stuns me.
You claim it in the name of piety.
Unlock these doors, hands off the lad's gold.
Show some sign of decency, hit the road.
Leave this house in peace, act the honest man,
Spare more trouble for this unhappy clan,
Beat your retreat –

Tartuffe

Kind sir, it's half-past three.
A goodly task is soon awaiting me.
Excuse me leaving you so rapidly.

Exit Tartuffe.

Cleante

So –

Enter Dorine, Mariane, Elmire.

Dorine

For God's sake, help me with Mariane.
The child will die if we don't thwart this plan.
All could be lost this very evening.
Let's work as one, please – look out, he's coming.
Put our heads together – we have the brains,
Prevent the master inflicting such pain.

Enter Orgon.

Orgon

Such a delight to find you gathered here.

He speaks to Mariane.

Daughter, this contract makes matters clear –

Mariane is on her knees.

Mariane

The heavens above know what I suffer.
Soften your hard heart towards me, Father.
Let my lot be more than one long lament.
To you I have always been obedient.
You once gave me life, do not cause my death.
For I tell you now, were this my last breath,
I beg you, Father, grant what I implore.
You forbid me marry the man I adore.
He is every hope that I have cherished.
That is my earnest and most heartfelt wish.
Spare me the torment that you have planned –
Despair awaits me if I wed that man.

Orgon is moved.

Orgon

Be firm, my heart – show no human weakness.

Mariane

You do as you believe is for the best.
Give him all you own, give all I own too.
I happily hand it over to you.
Do not include myself along with it.
Send me to a convent, there I can sit
And bear the remainder of my sad days,
Weeping to myself as I mourn and pray.

Orgon

This is what cruel daughters can become
When they lose respect for our religion.

Your heart hates receiving these attentions,
But you will soon be reading your wedding banns.

Dorine

But I heard –

Orgon

Quiet – from you I want not one word –

Cleante

Orgon, calm down – it makes sense to think twice.
May I dare offer you a bit of advice?

Orgon

Who could resist you, the voice of reason?
Well, for once in my life, I'll be the one.

Elmire speaks to her husband.

Elmire

What can I say, seeing what I see?
All you have to offer is fiddle-de-dee?
What kind of witchcraft does this man practise?
Why are you entranced – it is in his kiss?

Orgon

I know you spoil my scoundrel of a son.
You're in on his tricks, you know he's a con.
You're scared to say boo against all he mocks.
Poor man Tartuffe, did you even look shocked
At the appalling things said into his face?
You might have shown sympathy when that took place.

Elmire

An excuse for a man displays his wares –
He confides his love, and who the hell cares?
A hand finds its way crawling up a dress,
No point turning into people possessed.
I break my heart laughing at this nonsense,
Like something you'd see inside circus tents.
Who are these females red in tooth and claw

Who'll not stoop to conquer folly and flaw?
The wrong word could leave your cheeks in ribbons.
Jesus protect me from such odd wisdom.
You know how to make the strongest man balk?
Deliver a perfect punch to his cock.

Orgon
I know what to do, don't get in my way.

Elmire
For this man you'd believe black is white –
I stand amazed you cannot see the light.
What if I made you see the true Tartuffe?

Orgon
The true Tartuffe?

Elmire
I give you living proof –

Orgon
Nonsense.

Elmire
Show him as he is, lying toad.

Orgon
I'd not believe you – get out of my road.

Elmire
Say you hide yourself and could not be seen,
Under a table or behind a screen,
You yourself have full view of his action.
What would you make of this son of a gun?

Orgon
I would say nothing, it's not possible –

Elmire
You think not? I've another tale to tell.
Too long you've let yourself be deluded.
Your accusations would waken the dead –

Too long you've pointed the finger at me.
Cards on the table, what will be will be –
You'll learn what's what without further ado,
That man's long enlisted in Satan's crew.

Orgon
Let's see how crafty a picture you paint.
You're making a demon out of a saint.

Elmire
Ask him to come.

Dorine
                                His mind's like a scissors,
Sharp as daylight, he knows every score.

Elmire
Love can make eejits out of one and all.
Better men have drooped at vanity's call.
Tell him to come down now –

Exit Dorine.
    Elmire talks to Cleante and Mariane.

                                        And leave, you pair.

Exit Cleante, Mariane.

Elmire
Move this table, you need to get under.

Orgon
What? Where?

Elmire
                                We have to hide you, this minute.

Orgon
Under the table?

Elmire
                        Don't be a pain, do it.
I'm scheming and dreaming, judge me later.

Get beneath this, and hang on to your hair.
Don't be seen – don't be heard, I'm warning you.

Orgon

We had best see this operation through –
I think I'm being most obliging here –

Elmire

Right now, fast foot forward, no need to sneer.
What I say, what I do – pay it no heed.
You must allow me to follow my lead.
This is all to convince you, as promised.
Are you happy I'm now reduced to this?
Flatter him, though, he'll do as I ask.
I'll get the hypocrite to drop his mask –
Let the creep think his joy is unconfined.
Me give it to him? Last thing on my mind.
For you, you alone, I will confound him.
When you believe me, I'll stop the bounder.
Decide for yourself how far I should go –
You can put a stop to this Romeo.
Step in and save your poor wife's modesty.
You do believe me it's your best interest?
He's coming – be still, don't utter a peep.

Enter Tartuffe.

Tartuffe

You wanted a word – well, talk is cheap.

Elmire

I have some secrets that need revealing.
Come near to me, this canary will sing.
That bad boy Damis had me terrified,
You saw me pretend to be on his side.
I did not challenge his threats and his boasts.
Just as well – the pup, he's now cleared the coast.
Everything will work out for the better.
We can wallow in the law and the letter.

Because of him, none suspect a thing now.
Let's face it, you're my husband's sacred cow.
He cannot think any ill about you.
Can you credit what he wants you to do?
He wants us to be together at all times –
Let wagging tongues wag, we'll glide through the slime.
Here on our own, we can be safe and sound.
I open my heart – a hare to your hound.
Perhaps I'm too keen, a little too forward,
Have I said too much, are you on your guard?

Tartuffe

I'm finding this heart-to-heart quite hard.
A big change since last time you marked my card.

Elmire

Little you know how a woman's mind works.
Who knows where danger and destruction lurk?
Magnificent, strange, changeable beings,
We like you to nod when we pull the strings.
We want men to fall for our lovely charms,
But it takes a while to roll in our arms.
The eyes in our faces, what they give away,
Not the same as words our tight lips convey.
Accept, refuse, all matters of honour –
Such contradictions, could you ask for more?
Forgive my frankness, is it indecent?
Can you misunderstand what I always meant?
At long last now I can speak openly –
Forget all his threats – just forget Damis.
Your most gentle heart, that was your offer –
Something so special, tender and rare.
Yes, I refused, with such reluctance –
What else could I do in my circumstance?
Now I will see you hitched to Mariane.
I am in despair, cruel, cruel man.
Will you leave me wallowing in despair?
When it comes to your heart, I will not share.

Tartuffe

The lips I love give me purest honey,
Mellifluous, pure, fragrant and runny.
A sweetness I've never known before –
Such happiness pierces me right to the core.
Blessed are they who will spread it about,
But I must admit to this tiny doubt –
A complete change of heart – is it not odd?
Might you take me for a miserable sod
If I were to dare call into question
Your dulcet tones and their firm intentions
To convince me I should call off the wedding?
Might that be where your campaign is heading?
Should all you've just said lead me to believe,
No harm's been done, don't be so naïve,
I will get jam today, jam tomorrow?
To say this brings me no little sorrow,
Madame – I need a taste of your favours
For you to leave myself quite reassured
You mean what you say by my soul and yours.
I have a slight qualm it stinks of the sewer,
The charming attachment you say you feel.
I long and live in the hope that it's real.

Elmire coughs to alert her husband.

Elmire

Why the rush, my good man, what's with the speed?
It takes ages to cope with a woman's needs.
Would you have me list out my heart's demands?
Having confessed to you, aren't things grand?
But no, that's for nothing – that's not enough.
The rules of your game are dirty and rough.
Do I take it yourself won't be satisfied
Till the cows come home and the fish are fried?

Tartuffe

The less one deserves, the more one has to hope.
What are words but money for old rope?

Skilled in love, you can buy and sell with them.
I'm a hungry man, caged in his dark den,
And I have not earned what fate decrees,
A woman like you could never want me.
I still can't credit my excellent luck –
Delicate gazelle meets dirty big buck.
Where could I have you, country or city?
Don't you see my weakness – have you no pity?
Every bit of yourself I'm dying to lick.
Jesus, give us a right rub of the relic.

Elmire

Choosing a woman, aren't you the tyrant?
My mind's upside down thinking what you want.
Your love has the charge of a raging bull.
It can ride roughshod which way it will pull.
I cannot elude you – I can barely breathe.
You'll lay me in my coffin covered with wreaths.
Do you think it the task of a gentleman
To seize and grab hold of a lady's frail fan?
Do you think it right to take advantage
When a woman teeters at the very edge?
Do you not accept my weakness for you?

Tartuffe

Then why refuse the way that you do?
Look at me more kindly, spare one soft glance –

Elmire

How can I consent to whatever you want
And not offend God, His mother as well?

Tartuffe

That's all restrains you? Shake a leg, ring a bell –
No worries there – soon be home safe and dry,
No fear from that charge, no fear we might fry.
There are ways and means to humour heaven.
Ten commandments, round them down to seven.
I am well versed encouraging scruples.

I let conscience hatch from its shell
All ways and means of finding atonement,
Stretching the limits of all sacraments.
Actions may be evil, intentions pure –
That does the trick, your salvation is sure.
Be guided by me, you'll have yourself made.
Gratify my desire, don't be afraid.
That cough – it sounds bad –

Elmire

                        I'm in agony –

Tartuffe

Some liquorice juice – is your throat dry?

Elmire

A most stubborn cold – it has me quaking.

Tartuffe

Most unfortunate – it's left you shaking.

Elmire

More than I could say –

Tartuffe

Still, luck's come our way.
We're quite safe here, no one squeals or shouts,
The only crime lies in being found out.
Scandal is silly – what point when we win?
To sin, in secret, that is not to sin.

Elmire coughs more.

Elmire

That's it – what can I do but defer?
All that you claim, it's yours to declare.
Anything less, it would do a man down
With his God-given right to wear the crown
And claim what's in his legal ownership.
He rules the roost, and he cracks the whip.
It hurts my heart to step across this line.

I seem to be stuck where the sun won't shine.
I'll wander aimless, lost inside the dark,
Reduced to this with neither bite nor bark.
Harden myself, do the necessary –
If that leaves me the talk of the country,
Too bad for him forced me make a choice.
He is to blame, will be the people's voice.

Tartuffe

I shoulder all the blame –

Elmire

                    Step out and see
If my husband's in the hall looking for me?

Tartuffe

What need for us to take any notice?
How long since he shot the last of his fizz?
We could lead that blockhead round by the nose.
At my command he drops into a doze.
He falls for each and every single lie.
I have it so he won't believe his eyes.

Elmire

Still, go out and check if he's on the prowl.

Exit Tartuffe.

Orgon

Did you ever step in some dung more foul?
That rotten, filthy – he had me quite stunned.
Hook, line and sinker, he robbed me for fun.

Elmire

Up from there so quick – what are you doing?
Get back beneath the cloth, or you will swing.
It's not time yet, wait till the very end,
Beware the noble nature of your friend.
Learn for yourself, don't rely on tell-tales –

Orgon

Has more evil ever shot out from hell?

Elmire

Just hold your horse, let the truth sink in.
Watch how much you lose when that louse wins.
Be certain of his crimes, make no mistake.

Tartuffe comes back in.

Tartuffe

We are alone, good fortune's on the make.
The world is ours, according to my word.
My soul doth magnify my lady – lord.

Orgon

Easy there, less of the old *amore*.
Don't lose the run of yourself entirely.
You'd pull a fast one, praying on your knees,
You thought me green as the leaves on the trees,
And me, I fell for all your deceiving –
Would you say it's on the cards you're leaving?
You'd marry my daughter and desire my wife.
I would not listen, though rumours were rife.
You wolfed down the sweet fruits of temptation.
You'll never have luck for what you have done.
I could overhear your last bout of sweet talk –
The soft, cooing dove turned into a hawk.
If I need proof, you could not be kinder,
That's it, kaput, there is nothing further.

Elmire

They're not in my nature – lies of this sort.

Tartuffe

What? You believe –

Orgon

That's it – or I'll see you in court.
Get out of my house, nothing more to add.

Go – or will I hurl you out, devious lad?
You must leave, you heard me, I told you go.

Tartuffe

This house belongs to me, I'll have you know.
You're not who you think you are – the master.
You've brought on yourself utter disaster.
No use resorting to the coward's way –
I have means to make your greasy gang pay.
I have taken count of all your insults.
All that happens now comes down to your fault.
I have read the future – I know what it meant,
Heaven calling, repent, repent, repent.

Exit Tartuffe.

Act Five

Elmire
He's talking about –

Orgon
No laughing matter.

Elmire
Are you telling me he is our master?

Orgon
I was doing –

Elmire
You were doing –

Orgon
My best.
So I gave Tartuffe –

Elmire
You gave Tartuffe?

Orgon
A bequest.

Elmire
A bequest?

Orgon
It pains my soul –

Elmire
What pains your soul?

Orgon

The done deal.
There might be something even worse I feel.

Elmire

What?

Orgon

You'll find out soon enough. Check upstairs.

Elmire

What for?

Orgon

A strongbox.

Elmire

What's in it?

Orgon

That's what I fear.
What's in it might cause some hurly-burly.
Tartuffe has me by the short and curlies.
Do you know where we'd locate a magic wand?

Elmire

What have you done, poor fool of a husband?

Enter Cleante.

Cleante

Why the upheaval? What's the newest panic?

Elmire

Orgon has dumped us in the worst of his fixes.
There's a box –

Cleante

What box?

Orgon

My friend, Argas, locked –

Elmire
Argas, the complete and total header –

Cleante
Picks fights with shadows, goes hell for leather –

Orgon
A man to never, never ever trust –

Elmire
What did you give him?

Orgon
My eternal trust.

Elmire
Give me strength –

Cleante
In this box, debts and writs?

Orgon
Dangerous documents, crammed with state secrets.

Elmire
Argas, he has done the dirty once again.

Orgon
I took pity on a man in deep pain.
He gave it to me on peril of my soul.
What it contained was more precious than gold.
Private revelations, papers of import,
His property, his life, all mine to sort.

Cleante
Guard them as you would have guarded your life.
What harm have you done to you and your wife?
In this land the King is King – all know this.
Walls have ears and windows eyes, nothing's missed.
Why let the box fall into Tartuffe's hands?

Orgon

> Fear – I was in flitters – please understand,
> My conscience was playing pure blue murder.
> Had I done the right thing? I asked the bugger –
> Tartuffe said could he put it in his knapsack?
> If there were problems, he'd take the rap, Jack.
> I would not be caught out telling lies.
> I would have to give no false testimony.

Cleante

> Now that Tartuffe has power over you,
> He'll control all you say and all you do.
> You should have played things more cleverly –

Orgon

> How could I not fall for Tartuffe's sincerity?
> His heart, damaged goods – his soul, pure evil.
> A beggar on horseback, rotted, riddled.
> Me, I took him in, gave him his start.
> Well, I wash my hands of the pure of heart.
> Should they ever knock at my front door,
> I'll open and answer as Lucifer.

Cleante

> There you go, flying off the handle.
> Just try keeping to what's called an even keel.
> What point throwing yourself from pillar to post?
> It's clear what's right, why do the opposite?
> You see how it worked, his sham piety –
> He was the organ grinder, you his monkey.
> You know what I mean – it's been done before.
> Will you now make an even greater error?
> A scoundrel robs you both north and south,
> Acting the martyr, playing the poor mouth.
> Don't fall for more nonsense, act sensibly –
> Learn to appreciate true piety.

> *Enter Damis.*

Damis

The coward shows he's foul as he's vile?
His pride hides beneath his spotless smile.
This is how he rewards you, my good father?

Orgon

He does – where do I turn, son, tell me where?
He has ripped my heart out –

Damis

                       I'll cut off his ears.
I knew he was never what he appeared.

Cleante

Manners, and restraint, young man, they're the thing –
Cast aside violence, respect our king.

Enter Pernelle, Filipote, Dorine.

Pernelle

What's happening? I've heard bad tidings –

Orgon

You'll find out which way the pendulum swings.
See the rewards I reap for my charity.
Look on the blessings my cares showered on me.
I take a destitute in from the streets.
He devours my house and hand for his meat.
My daughter, my chattels – he'll have them for life.
That's not sufficient, he'd claw my wife.
He sees fit to threaten me for my good deeds –
In order to ruin me he now proceeds
To use the advantage my kind heart allowed –
Leave me in penury – do himself proud.
The beggar and thief is gentleman now.

Dorine

Poor soul.

Pernelle

             Such wickedness he'd not commit –

Orgon
How do –

Pernelle
Virtue brings the vicious out in fits.

Orgon
What are you trying to say, Mother?

Pernelle
You know I think your home an open sewer –
A sin bin for sodomites and whores.
Treating him in this most undeserving way –

Orgon
Mother, have you heard a single word I say?

Pernelle
When you were a lad, above all seen and heard,
I warned you beware of the bitter word.
You know as well as I do lies have legs.

Orgon
I see it myself, hence I'm in a rage –

Pernelle
Tie not round your neck millstones of scandal.

Orgon
This woman, my mother, she'll drive me to hell.
With my own two eyes, I witnessed his crime –

Pernelle
None can halt the charge of the devil's swine.
Nothing in this world can offer defence –

Orgon
To me this talk makes absolutely no sense.
I saw him – saw him with my own two eyes.
Do I have to declare it from the mountain high?

Pernelle

Where even sweet Jesus felt temptation.
Feel the agony of Our Father's son.
It's human nature to tread warily.
Sometimes it's best to just wait and see –

Orgon

So a man lets his wife be manhandled,
That's now to be found scrawled in the Bible?

Pernelle

Accept in good faith the word of your brother,
Have some cause before you accuse others.

Orgon

How can I heap this higher on your plate?
Bring the pair in and let them demonstrate –

Pernelle

That lamb is as wholesome as he is bonny.
I will not entertain your calumny.

Exit Pernelle, Filipote.

Orgon

Look at my mother, the eejit in the hat,
If she pushes me further, I'll knock her flat.

Dorine

You'd not believe us – now he's got you beaten.
The way of the world, sir: eat or be eaten.

Cleante

We're wasting time – stop this chatter.
Better take care of this urgent matter.
The man's an infidel – he knows no limits.

Damis

You think he would serve us with his writs?

Elmire

He has no case, look at the evidence,
His ingratitude is our best defence –

Cleante

Don't bank on that – this boy is wily.
He'll stick in the knife, served with a smile.
People find themselves in sticky situations,
Their accusers have lots to go on.
He's armed with what I'd call your smoking gun.
To deal with his like always best turn and run.

Orgon

Easy to be wise after the event.
He had my heart scalded, my back was bent –

Cleante

Why can't you shake hands – say peace be with you?
No chance to patch things up between the two?

Elmire

I would have let fleas and sleeping dogs lie
If I'd known he could blind us in both eyes.

Orgon turns to Dorine.

Orgon

Who's that hovering – what does he want here?
I'm in no state to be handing out cheer.

Enter Monsieur Loyal.

Monsieur Loyal

I salute you, girl, in the name of Christ,
A word with your master would suffice.

Dorine

No callers allowed – up to his elbows.

Monsieur Loyal

I assure you I am no vexatious fellow.
I am a harbinger of mirth and glee.
The reason I'm here will make him happy.

Dorine

Name?

Monsieur Loyal

Tell him I'm here, Tartuffe sent me – Tartuffe.
That's the man asked me under his roof.

Dorine

A man's here, on Tartuffe's business, he claims,
Very civil –

Cleante

What does he want? What is his name?

Orgon

He might suggest we can be reconciled.

Cleante

Then do nothing rash – nothing wild.
If that's his mission, you must listen –

Monsieur Loyal

God protect you and yours above all men.
I wish every blessing upon your head.
I bid you joy and every Godspeed.

Orgon

This bodes well for a happy accord,
I give you, good sir, the warmth of my word –

Monsieur Loyal

I know your family's respectability,
I honour your father's noble history.

Orgon

Sir, forgive my ignorance, who might you be –

Monsieur Loyal

Loyal by name, from noble Normandy.
Thanks be to God these past forty years,
Winding my way through this valley of tears,
I've served as Bailiff with much honour due.
That's why, sir, by your leave, I come to you
Bearing a writ, legal notification –

Orgon
What?

Monsieur Loyal
A notice, sir, what needs to be done.
An order you leave here, all you and yours,
Make room for others – remove furniture
Without further ado or more delay.

Orgon
Leave my home?

Monsieur Loyal
This instant, this very day.
This house now belongs to Monsieur Tartuffe.
He prays not to seem hasty nor uncouth,
But he is master of your possessions,
Lord of your estate, see it writ in stone –
In contract form, I have it here with me.
No disputing what the world plainly sees.

Damis
I stand amazed – this is some impudence.

Monsieur Loyal
My business concerns this man of good sense.
I'll deal with him, both reasonable and mild.
He conducts himself better than some spoilt child
Kicking – screaming – in the face of justice.

Orgon
But –

Monsieur Loyal
Sir, that would not be your way to resist.
I just take one look and I'm certain it's true,
All the money in the world could not tempt you
To do the dirty and put up a fight
Against what you know is perfectly right.
I'm here to carry out the orders given –
I will do so in the name of heaven.

Damis
> You're looking for a hiding black and blue
> In your mourning garb –

Monsieur Loyal
>   No credit to you,
> Sir – get him to hold his tongue and leave.
> I do not intend to cause you more grief,
> I'd hate to name you as cause for complaint.

Dorine (*aside*)
> Loyal by name, but by nature he ain't.

Monsieur Loyal
> I am known for my benevolent strain,
> I took on this service to avoid you pain.
> To oblige and please were my intention.
> Show a bit of mannerly care, unlike some –
> Their manner might be less agreeable.
> They mock the life of the families that flee.

Orgon
> You bar my windows as you empty my purse,
> You chase me from my home – what could be worse?

Monsieur Loyal
> We're giving you stay of execution.
> Look on the bright side while the deal's being done.
> I'll be back tonight with my ten strong men.
> As a matter of form, I must be given
> The keys to your door before you go to bed.
> Don't let any of this bother your head.
> I'll mind this nest as if it were my own.
> But leave the place empty, picked clean as a bone.
> Plonk everything outside – rely on my lads.
> They'll lend a helping hand – they'll be glad.
> Now I'm doing you a big favour.
> I hope for the same from you and yours.
> Behave yourselves – let me do my duty.

Orgon
    I'd consider it a sublime beauty
    To leave my fist's imprint on that ugly gob.
    What about it, son, are we up to the job?

Damis
    Hold me back, Father – I'm only itching –

Cleante
    Stop, the pair of you –

Dorine turns on Monsieur Loyal.

Dorine
                        Your backbone's mitching –
    Monsieur Loyal, wish I had a big stick –

Monsieur Loyal
    Girl, enough of your folderols and tricks.
    The law's strict on women as well as men.

Cleante
    You're overflown with threats, learn to say when.
    Give me the document – and leave us at once, please.

Monsieur Loyal
    Goodbye, God grant you His comfort and peace.

Orgon
    May all belonging to you die roaring –

Exit Monsieur Loyal.
    Enter Pernelle, Filipote.

    Look who's arrived on a prayer and a wing?
    Is it my perfect mother of sorrows?
    Where stands she now – how does her garden grow?
    His writs, his betrayals, his thieving, his lies –
    What say you, Mother – have we opened your eyes?

Pernelle

Son, I am too steeped in shame, I am stunned.
Let me at last admit all the wrongs I've done –

Dorine

Tell me, what right now have you to complain?
This paragon, this angel without stain,
He knew that money might well destroy a man,
So he robbed you blind as part of God's plan.
He freed you from all worldly excess –

Orgon

For once in your life would you give it a rest?

Cleante

We should go see what advice to follow.

Elmire

His foul ways and misdemeanours can't go
Without the whole world marking down his card.
There's ways and means of hitting him hard.
The law won't allow him to laugh in our face.

Enter Valere.

Valere

A pressing danger hurries me to this place.
Whatever you say, say nothing for sure –
I know a man who owes me big favours –
All very delicate and very hush-hush,
He is on our case – without further gush.
He's sent me warning you should leave straightaway,
Without looking back, no further delay.
The swindler who pulled and tangled your strings
Denounced you an hour ago to the great King.
He's passed on a strongbox which he maintains
Belongs to this country's most vicious villain.
You kept this casket a guilty secret.
Such behaviour, sir, is indeed most ill-met.
I don't know the precise name for your crime,

But a warrant's coming in next to no time.
Tartuffe himself, he'll do the delivery –
Hold him back, I'd say, the lump of misery.

Cleante

The worm turns in no uncertain manner.
He claims all you have to crown himself master.

Orgon

The man's a beast – a boiled brute of a beast.

Valere

We've no time for even a moment's rest.
The slightest delay for you is fatal.
Take these thousand crowns – they come from a pal –
This is a rough one, but waste no more time,
You have to take to your heels – your path's mine.
I offer my service to you as a friend.
I will walk beside you till the very end.

Orgon

How can I thank you, my most near, most dear?
Your kindness moves me to these heartfelt tears.
I'll beg the heavens show my gratitude,
For this noble service, I will do you good –
You will be rewarded as you should.

Enter Tartuffe with Arresting Officer.

Tartuffe

Ever generous and ever gentle,
Allow me lead my lord to the prison cell –
I arrest you in the name of the Crown.

Orgon

So this is how you will haul me down?
Here's the blow against me you've saved till last?
You mock me now for my kindness in the past.

Tartuffe

Heaven has taught me how to tolerate
Scandalous insults and the barbs of hate.

Cleante

Such modesty, sir, does you great credit –

Damis

Mock heaven, scoundrel, your bowels will split –

Tartuffe

I think of nothing but doing my duty –
Your blasts of anger, what matter to me?

Mariane

You're a man of most revered profession.
Are you proud the world regards you as scum?

Tartuffe

What can I do but delight when I confess
I must be about my Father's business?

Orgon

You watched my hand give, you waited and bit –

Tartuffe

I know what assistance I received from it.
The King, the King, that's my rallying cry,
He is my first, my only sacred duty –
I would sacrifice and cast aside
Friends, wife, family, to the coming tide.

Elmire

Hypocrite.

Cleante

You tried to seduce this lady –
Does that not seem to all just a tad shady?
When did you think fit to denounce the man –
When he stopped you greasing your palm?
Far be it from me to deter you doing good,

Your conscience must declare as you should.
You received the gift of all his estate.
Give back those soiled goods – do not hesitate.

Tartuffe turns to the Arresting Officer.

Tartuffe
Sir, spare me from this whinging, I pray –

Arresting Officer
We're taking too long, let's settle this today.
You do well to remind me move swiftly
And implement the order, follow me –
I'll lead you where you'll die in prison.

Tartuffe
Me, sir?

Arresting Officer
      You, yes.

Tartuffe
            Me, die? Give me an explanation –

Arresting Officer
Not to you.

The Arresting Officer turns to Orgon.

      Calm yourself, sir, you're so afraid,
But our King is an enemy to fraud.
His love does not blind him to what's vicious.
Tartuffe has long made the King suspicious.
He's dealt with better and with worse knaves
And sent them packing to unholy graves.
Accusing you, Tartuffe gave his game away.
The swindler knows he will truly rue the day
He's revealed himself a notorious crook
Who plied his trade under another hook.
He's committed a long list of dark deeds
Which could fill volumes for the country to read.

The King loathed his ungrateful disloyalty.
I must divest Tartuffe of your property,
Return to you papers in his possession,
Invalidate gifts of your estate at once.
Your friend who slipped our security nets –
The King pardons this breach of state secrets.
He knows how to reward services rendered.
He shows his heart is most wise and tender.
He knows what is due to all his citizens.
He has the measure of all women and men.

Orgon

Would you say, scoundrel, this is to your liking?
It is all down to the King's own doings.

Tartuffe

Beware of your friends in the highest places.
Beware of their hundred thousand faces.
Burn me, brand me, I will declare one thing,
In this land of lies the liar is king.

Cleante

Do not mock those that are unfortunate.
Pity the man suffering his sad fate.
Pray instead his soul returns to the true way
So that the King softens his harsh penalty.
Praise the Lord, we who are all carved from dust.
Bend and genuflect now, all of us.

Arresting Officer

The King, the King, that's our rallying cry.
He is our first, our only sacred duty.
His eyes can penetrate the minds of men.
He sorts the guilty from the innocent.
Nothing leads his soul into error.
He loathes hypocrites and all imposters.
His great soul's gift of fine discernment
Rewards reason, serene and heaven-sent.

He bestows his glory on the worthy.
His favour heeds neither blood nor birth.

Orgon
Let us go and praise his goodness and joy,
But first I must turn to this girl and boy.
I wish you in Eden, sweet Mariane.
Valere, I permit you, take her hand.
Be wed in bliss, as all true lovers are.
May your love outlast the sun, moon and stars.